LAW

Lawton, Val
West Virginia

34880000823752

WEST VIRGINIA

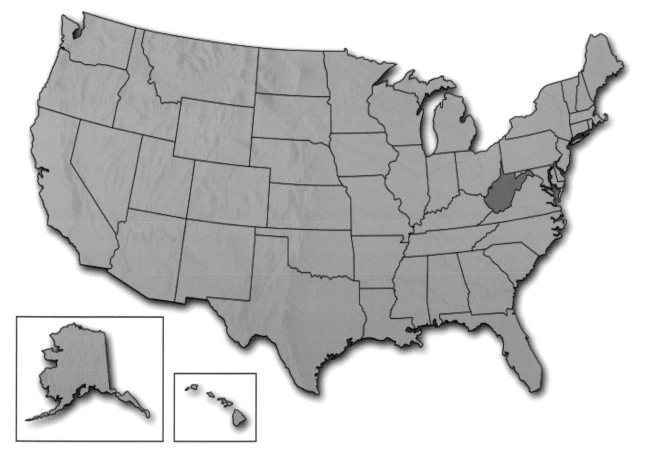

Val Lawton

Published by Weigl Publishers Inc.
123 South Broad Street, Box 227
Mankato, MN   56002
USA
Web site: http://www.weigl.com

Library of Congress Cataloging-in-Publication Data

Lawton, Val.
    West Virginia / Val Lawton.
         p. cm. -- (A kid's guide to American states)
    Includes bibliographical references (p.) and index.
    ISBN 1-930954-58-1 (lib. bdg.)
     1. West Virginia--Juvenile literature. [1. West Virginia.] I. Title. II. Series.

F241.3 .L39 2001
975.4--dc21

                                               2001026142
ISBN 1-930954-02-6 (pbk.)

Printed in the United States of America
1 2 3 4 5 6 7 8 9 10   05 04 03 02 01

Project Coordinator
Michael Lowry
Substantive Editor
Rennay Craats
Copy Editor
Heather Kissock
Designers
Warren Clark
Terry Paulhus
Layout
Bryan Pezzi
Photo Researcher
Diana Marshall

Photograph Credits

Every reasonable effort has been made to trace ownership and to obtain
permission to reprint copyright material. The publishers would be
pleased to have any errors or omissions brought to their attention so
that they may be corrected in subsequent printings.

Cover: Man in doorway of West Virginian cabin (© Kevin Fleming/CORBIS), Trees in
autumn (Corbis); **Augusta Heritage Center:** pages 22T, 22B; **Berkeley County
Historical Society:** page 19B; **Charleston Convention & Visitors Bureau:** pages 6T,
15T, 21T, 21BR; **Corbis Corporation:** page 15BL; **Corel Corporation:** pages 10B, 20T,
28T, 29B; **EyeWire Corporation:** page 28B; **Jay Hurley:** page 29T; **Jamboree
USA/Jamboree In the Hills:** page 24T; **Kirkwood Winery:** page 15BR; **PhotoDisc,
Inc.:** page 20BL; **Photofest:** pages 24BR, 25T, 25B, 26B; **Stephen J. Shaluta Jr.:** pages
5BL, 7BL, 11MR, 13B, 16B, 19BL, 24BL, 27TR; **Van Slider:** pages 4T, 4B, 6BL, 8T, 14T,
21BL; **Ron Snow/West Virginia Division of Natural Resources:** pages 3T, 6BR, 7BR,
8BL, 8BR, 10T, 11ML, 11B, 12BL, 12BR, 20BR, 27B; **West Virginia Development
Office:** page 13T; **West Virginia Division of Culture and History/Archives and
History Section:** pages 18T, 18B, 19T; **West Virginia Division of Tourism:** pages 3M,
3B, 4BL, 7T, 9T, 9B, 12T, 14B, 23TR, 23B, 26T, 27TL; **West Virginia Italian Heritage
Festival:** page 23M; **Marilyn "Angel" Wynn:** pages 16T, 17TR, 17M, 17B; **Yeager
Airport:** page 5T.

CONTENTS

INTRODUCTION

The Glade Creek Grist Mill continues to grind flour using traditional methods. The mill is one of West Virginia's most recognized landmarks.

"Almost heaven, West Virginia!" That is how singer and songwriter John Denver felt about the state of West Virginia. It is no wonder, for West Virginia is home to spectacular scenery, beautiful farms, and misty rolling hills. It also has a rich history and culture, which makes visiting the state a rewarding and memorable experience.

West Virginia is known for its unique **rural** mountain culture. Since their mountain location was quite isolated, early West Virginians developed a local culture that was uninfluenced by neighboring populations. Many of these mountain traditions, such as folk songs and storytelling, still exist today.

QUICK FACTS

The state motto is *Montani semper liberi*, which means "mountaineers are always free."

West Virginia has the highest mean altitude of any state east of the Mississippi River—1,500 feet.

West Virginia was admitted to the Union in 1863 as the thirty-fifth state.

The state flower is the rhododendron, also known as the big laurel.

September and October are beautiful months in West Virginia, as forest-covered hillsides come alive with splendid fall colors.

Getting There

West Virginia is nestled between Pennsylvania and Maryland on the north, Virginia on the east and the south, and Kentucky and Ohio on the west. The Ohio River forms the border between Ohio and West Virginia. One of the Ohio River's **tributaries**, the Potomac River, forms West Virginia's northern border with Maryland.

Drivers in West Virginia take advantage of the more than 37,370 miles of road that cross the state. About 550 miles of these roads are interstate highways. For those who prefer to fly, West Virginia has sixty-five airports to serve travelers. Yeager Airport, near Charleston, is West Virginia's busiest airport.

The Yeager Airport is named in honor of Charles Yeager, the first person to fly faster than the speed of sound.

West Virginia Location Map

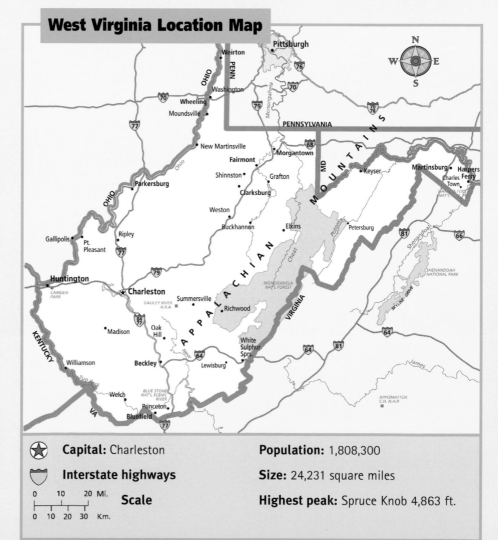

Pittsburgh
Weirton
OHIO
PENN
Washington
Wheeling
Moundsville
PENNSYLVANIA
New Martinsville
Morgantown
Fairmont
Shinnston
Grafton
Parkersburg
Clarksburg
Ohio
Weston
Keyser
Martinsburg
Harpers Ferry Town
MD
MOUNTAINS
Buckhannon
Elkins
Petersburg
Gallipolis
Ripley
Pt. Pleasant
Huntington
CAMDEN PARK
Charleston
Summersville
GAULEY RIVER N.R.A.
Richwood
MONONGAHELA NAT'L FOREST
Cheat
Potomac
APPALACHIAN
SHENANDOAH NATIONAL PARK
Shenandoah
SKYLINE DRIVE
Madison
Oak Hill
White Sulphur Sprs.
VIRGINIA
New River
KENTUCKY
Williamson
Beckley
Lewisburg
James
Tug Fork
Welch
BLUE STONE NAT'L SCENIC RIVER
Princeton
Bluefield
VA
APPOMATTOX C.H. N.H.P.

★ **Capital:** Charleston

Interstate highways

0   10   20 Mi.   **Scale**
0 10 20 30 Km.

Population: 1,808,300

Size: 24,231 square miles

Highest peak: Spruce Knob 4,863 ft.

When Charleston was established in 1794, the total population was thirty-five people. The town itself was made up of only seven houses.

The capital of West Virginia is Charleston. It is located in Kanawha County, where the Elk and the Kanawha Rivers meet. It is the largest city in the state, with a population of about 55,000 people. Charleston is referred to as both the "most northern" of the southern cities and the "most southern" of the northern cities. Like all of the large West Virginian cities, Charleston is located in a river valley, where the land is flat.

Charleston has many historic buildings and grand mansions. Many of these landmarks date back to the late nineteenth century. Some say that Charleston is one of the country's most beautiful capital cities. West Virginia's other major cities are Huntington, Wheeling, Parkersburg, and Morgantown.

QUICK FACTS

The cardinal was chosen as the state bird in 1949.

The New River Gorge Bridge has the world's longest single steel arch. It is 3,030 feet long.

Both West Virginia and Virginia were named in honor of Elizabeth I, the Virgin Queen of England.

Illinois and South Carolina also have cities named Charleston.

The Victorian district in Wheeling is a sign of its prosperous past. During the 1800s, the city served as a major gateway to the west.

During the fall, battles from the American Civil War are re-enacted in several state parks across West Virginia.

Located in the middle of the Appalachian Mountains, West Virginia is the most mountainous state east of the Rocky Mountains. The state's unusual boundaries, created by mountains and rivers, give it the shape of a pan with two large handles. This shape inspired one of West Virginia's nicknames—"The Panhandle State."

West Virginia separated from the state of Virginia during the American Civil War. A series of disagreements between the eastern and western parts of Virginia caused the separation. The people of western Virginia wanted to have their own state. They felt unfairly taxed and believed that they were receiving few benefits. There was also growing tension over the issue of slavery. Many West Virginians were opposed to slave-owning, while wealthy eastern planters had many slaves. The new state was originally called "Kanawha," but the name "West Virginia" was later chosen.

QUICK FACTS

There are three official state songs: "West Virginia, My Home Sweet Home," "The West Virginia Hills," and "This is My West Virginia."

In 1859, John Brown raided the national armory at Harpers Ferry to get guns and ammunition for a slave rebellion. Though he was unsuccessful, this action was important to the growing anti-slavery movement in the United States.

The Seneca Rocks formation rises nearly 900 feet above the North Fork River. It is one of West Virginia's most visited natural sites.

West Virginia is known for its thick, rolling fog, which occurs around its many rivers and its high mountain ranges.

LAND AND CLIMATE

All of West Virginia lies within the geographic region known as the Appalachian Mountain System. This region extends from Vermont to Alabama. The state is further divided into two separate regions—the Allegheny Plateau and the Appalachian Ridge.

Much of West Virginia lies on the Allegheny Plateau. At the highest point of the plateau, the weather is severe and can change suddenly. Dense fogs can collect, and fierce winds often blow.

The Appalachian Ridge is made up of long mountain ridges, which are covered in forests. The Blue Ridge Mountains form the eastern edge of the Appalachian Ridge and are visible from the Eastern Panhandle.

West Virginia's climate tends to be humid. Rainfall averages between 40 to 60 inches per year, though more rain falls in the highlands. Average January temperatures in West Virginia range from 28° Fahrenheit to 38°F. July temperatures vary from 68°F to 76°F.

The Grandview Overlook offers a spectacular view of the New River.

NATURAL RESOURCES

West Virginia has many natural resources. It is among the nation's leading sources of **bituminous coal**, producing an estimated 180 million tons per year. Stone, cement, salt, and oil are also important resources for the state.

The oil and gas industry in West Virginia is linked to the salt industry. In the early 1800s, oil and gas were of little importance. Salt workers in the Kanawha Valley often struck oil or gas while drilling for salt. They thought it was a nuisance. Once the value of oil and natural gas was recognized, the region boomed in petroleum production.

For many years, West Virginia was the largest producer of natural gas east of the Mississippi River. The state still produces large amounts of natural gas in the Appalachian Basin. West Virginia produces about 178 billion cubic feet of natural gas and 1.5 million barrels of oil per year.

Fifty-three out of West Virginia's fifty-five counties contain coal.

West Virginia is ranked the third most-forested state in the nation. Many of its trees are used to make lumber.

QUICK FACTS

West Virginia has about 384 oil and gas fields.

The third-largest diamond ever found in the United States was uncovered at Peterstown.

Three-quarters of West Virginia, or 11.9 million acres, is covered in forests.

PLANTS AND ANIMALS

Unlike mountain ranges in the western United States, the Appalachians have deep soil in which many plants flourish. In Kanawha State Forest, visitors can find a wide variety of trees and plants. This includes twenty-three types of wild orchids and seven types of sunflowers. West Virginia is home to many flowering bushes, such as laurel, hepatica, wild geranium, and black-eyed Susan. Oak, maple, birch, and pine trees all grow in West Virginia.

Another region that stands out for its fertile soil and ideal climate is the valley of the New River. Over millions of years, the New River has moved many tons of rich **sediment** into its lower valley. As a result, the soil along the valley floor is ideal for growing plants and produces an abundant amount of lush vegetation.

West Virginia is home to more than 1 million acres of National forest.

QUICK FACTS

An important research center is located in West Virginia. The National Fisheries Center at Leetown conducts research on the effects of pollution and climate change on different types of fish.

Over the years, West Virginia's trees have been severely damaged by insects and disease. By 1926, nearly all of the state's chestnut trees had been destroyed by the **chestnut blight**.

In Cabwaylingo State Forest, trails lead through hardwood and hemlock forests, near fields of magnolias and wildflowers.

Researchers at Leetown's National Fisheries Center tag and monitor fish to help understand fish behavior.

Conservation efforts in West Virginia have helped many small animals to survive. These include skunks, opossums, and bobcats.

Opossum

West Virginia has many threatened or endangered animal species living within its borders. These include the peregrine falcon, the eastern cougar, and the Virginia big-eared bat.

In the area around Bluestone State Park, blue herons, kingfishers, bobcats, foxes, and wild turkeys can be seen in the woods. While many of West Virginia's larger mammals have disappeared from the state, deer and black bears can still be found in the high country. Trout, bass, and pike are found in West Virginia's streams and rivers.

West Virginia is also home to many different kinds of birds. Loons, ducks, and geese are **migratory** species. Quails, woodcocks, owls, eagles, and hawks also fly West Virginia's skies. The songs of the cardinal, wood thrush, brown thrasher, and scarlet tanager can be heard throughout the state.

Bluestone Lake is a popular tourist destination. More than 670,000 guests visit the park yearly.

Over the years, industrial development has taken over much of the deer's natural habitat. Many deer have been forced to graze on garden flowers found in rural towns.

TOURISM

Tourism is very important to West Virginia's economy. The state's natural beauty attracts visitors from across the country. There are plenty of outdoor activities to enjoy in West Virginia's nine state forests and thirty-five state parks, including fishing, river rafting, hiking, camping, and skiing. More than 1 million acres of West Virginian land is dedicated to parks.

The mineral springs are another popular attraction found throughout the state. The best known are those at Berkeley Springs and White Sulphur Springs. Berkeley Springs is the oldest spa in the country.

The largest tourist draw in West Virginia is Harpers Ferry National Historical Park. Visitors to the park are treated to some fascinating bits of United States history. The town of Harpers Ferry is the site of **abolitionist** John Brown's famous raid on a United States arsenal and armory. The armory had been one of the main suppliers of rifles for both the War of 1812 and the American Civil War.

The Gauley River National Recreation Area covers a 26-mile stretch of exciting white water. It is rated the second-best river for white-water rafting in North America.

QUICK FACTS

Visitors to West Virginia spend about $2.8 billion per year.

President George Washington and his wife Martha often visited Berkeley Springs.

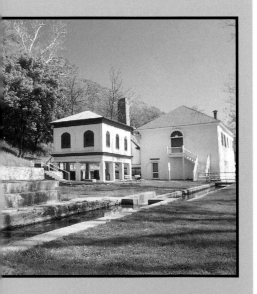

Jefferson Rock in the Shenandoah Valley was named for Thomas Jefferson, who helped survey the area as a young man.

The beautiful and historic Harpers Ferry is located at the point where the Potomac and Shenandoah Rivers meet.

The Toyota manufacturing plant, in Buffalo, West Virginia, employs about 700 workers to produce its engines and transmissions.

INDUSTRY

West Virginia's industries are based mainly on manufacturing and mining. Most years, West Virginia ranks third in coal production, contributing about 15 percent of the nation's total. West Virginia also mines limestone. The limestone bedrock **quarried** in the state is rich in calcium carbonate, potassium, and phosphorus. These elements make West Virginia lime an excellent fertilizer for farm pastures and lawns. Lime is also used for the production of steel.

Manufacturing is the most important activity for West Virginia's economy. The state's mineral resources are used to manufacture products in the chemical, glass, and high-technology industries.

Important manufacturing areas in West Virginia include the cities of Charleston, Huntington, and Parkersburg, along with the Kanawha River Valley. These areas are responsible for the production of **fabricated metals** and machinery.

Coal is West Virginia's major export. Deposits of coal are found under nearly 40 percent of the state.

West Virginia is home to more than 21,000 farms. The average farm is about 176 acres in size.

GOODS AND SERVICES

Large fruit orchards in West Virginia's Eastern Panhandle grow apples and peaches. Hay, wheat, oats, corn, and tobacco are the principal crops on West Virginian farms. Farmers also produce dairy products, and raise **broiler chickens** and cattle.

West Virginia's glass country can be found in the rolling hills of the Tri-State region, where Ohio, Kentucky, and West Virginia meet. Dozens of companies make beautiful glass products, using the state's sand deposits. Many **artisans** in this region make handmade and blown glassware, and offer glassmaking demonstrations to visitors.

QUICK FACTS

The first government owned parking building in the United States was opened on September 1, 1941, in Welch. It could hold 232 cars and showed a profit in its very first year.

The types of glass made in West Virginia include stained glass, plate glass, and tableware.

The most common farms in West Virginia are livestock farms.

West Virginian miners often own farms to make extra money. Farmland makes up about one-quarter of West Virginia's total land area.

The Brooke Glass Company has been manufacturing glass since 1879. Their specialties include hand-painted lamps, lamp parts, and giftware.

Downtown Charleston draws many tourists with its entertainment, market shops, and trolley-bus rides.

West Virginia has a small but exciting wine industry. The southern and central highland valleys grow wonderful wine-making grapes such as Concord, Niagara, and French **hybrids** called Seyval, Foch, and Vidal Blanc. Until the mid-1980s, winemaking was only done on a very small scale. Now the West Virginian government allows the sale of wines produced on large farms.

More than 28 percent of West Virginian workers have jobs in the service industry. Some of these jobs are with the government, hospitals, and public transit. Tourism is an important part of the service industry in West Virginia. Nearly 84,000 West Virginians are employed in the tourist industry. Some of these people work in restaurants, hotels, and tourist attractions.

QUICK FACTS

West Virginia's first winery opened in the Kanawha Valley in 1856.

Since the 1960s, a number of federal offices and facilities have been built in West Virginia. Government service is a growing employment area.

Software Valley, an area between Morgantown and Clarksburg, is home to a number of computer software companies.

The Kirkwood Winery hosts the Kirkwood Grape Stomping festival on the third weekend in September of each year. Visitors crush grapes with their feet in this winemaking tradition.

Paleo-Indian tools were used to grind berries, nuts, and plants when preparing food.

FIRST NATIONS

The first people in West Virginia were the Paleo-Indians. These early hunters lived in the area between 8,000 and 10,000 years ago. **Archeologists** have found their stone tools in the Kanawha and Ohio Valleys. The Paleo-Indians were often on the move and never permanently settled in the area.

Later, several different cultures settled in West Virginia's Northern and Eastern Panhandles. There, archeologists have uncovered tools, pottery, and ceremonial burial grounds. Most of these remains are from the Adena and Hopewell cultures. They built large ceremonial mounds for which they earned the name "Mound Builders." The Grave Creek Mound, in Marshall County, is the largest mound in the United States. It is 62 feet high and 240 feet in diameter. Archeologists believe that it was built between 250 BC and 150 BC.

QUICK FACTS

The Grave Creek Mound was accidentally discovered by Europeans in 1770, when a settler fell off the top of it while hunting.

To protect Native-American land claims, England's King George III issued the Proclamation of 1763. It stated that no one could settle west of the Allegheny Mountains. Many people, including George Washington, disobeyed the king's orders and claimed large areas of what is now West Virginia for themselves.

The Grave Creek Mound was a massive undertaking. The Adena had to move more than 60,000 tons of earth in basket loads.

The city and county of Logan are named for Logan, chief of the Mingo. Mingo County is named after this group.

Chief Logan was a friend to the new settlers, but became their bitter enemy when his family was killed by a group of European men.

Many Native-American groups, like the Shawnee, continued to oppose European settlement until the end of the eighteenth century.

By the 1600s, the Delaware and the Shawnee had moved into West Virginia. Around the same time, the Iroquois Confederacy began moving into the area. The Confederacy was an **alliance** of five Iroquois-speaking nations—Mohawk, Oneida, Onondaga, Cayuga, and Seneca. In 1722, the Tuscaroras joined the Iroquois Confederacy, and it became known as the Six Nations.

European exploration and settlement forced many Native Americans west. As a result of this forced migration, there was much tension and bloodshed in the seventeenth and eighteenth centuries. By the mid-1700s, the Iroquois began to give up their land claims in West Virginia through a series of **treaties**.

The Delaware called themselves the Lenni Lenape, which means "original people."

The Iroquois Confederacy had a common council, where chiefs voted on all decisions. The chiefs were elected to the council.

EXPLORERS AND MISSIONARIES

It is thought that the first European to see what is now West Virginia was John Lederer. Lederer and his group reached the top of the Blue Ridge Mountains, which bordered Virginia to the west. At the time, Lederer was exploring for Sir William Berkeley, the governor of Virginia. Lederer made a total of three trips to these mountains between 1669 and 1670.

The French and the British battled for nearly 100 years for control of the region. The discovery of the New River in 1671 was a turning point for the British. With access to the great river, the British could expand their power by laying claim to the entire Ohio Valley. The expedition that discovered this ancient river was called the Batts and Fallam Expedition. It allowed fur traders and explorers to move further west, into Virginia's wilderness. The British eventually defeated the French in the French and Indian War (1754–1763). The British then took over the area that is now West Virginia.

French claims to the West Virginia region were based on the voyages of René-Robert Cavelier, Sieur de La Salle.

QUICK FACTS

British explorers were the first to travel deep into West Virginia. In the 1670s, Thomas Batts and Robert Fallam were hired to find out if any of the rivers in the area drained into the Pacific Ocean.

Daniel Boone lived in West Virginia. He was a frontiersman and legendary hero who helped blaze a trail through Cumberland Gap.

Traveling ministers, called circuit riders, brought religion to isolated settlers. The most famous of these was Francis Asbury, who made thirty-four trips to West Virginia between 1776 and 1815.

Daniel Boone was a well-known trapper and pioneer. He lived in West Virginia at Point Pleasant from 1788 to 1798.

EARLY SETTLERS

The area now known as the Eastern Panhandle attracted West Virginia's early settlers. Colonel Morgan was West Virginia's first settler. He built his cabin in Berkeley County in the Eastern Panhandle. Morgan and his family moved from Delaware in 1730. Both Morgantown and Morgan County were named in the family's honor.

The Shenandoah Valley was a major southern migration route for Scottish, Irish, and German settlers. A large percentage of these pioneers came from the Pennsylvania and New Jersey colonies. Many settlers built homes along West Virginia's rivers, but few settled on the Allegheny Plateau. By 1800, West Virginia's population had risen to 78,000, most of which were farmers. They raised livestock and grew corn, wheat, and garden vegetables. Settlement in the region continued to grow as natural resources, such as coal and oil, were discovered.

Colonel Morgan's cabin was re-constructed in 1976, using as many of the logs from the original cabin as possible. Today, visitors to the cabin can experience what pioneer life was like during the early 1700s.

During the 1730s, land grants were given to settlers on the condition that they bring in one family for each 1,000 acres of land.

QUICK FACTS

German families established a settlement on the Potomac River in the 1730s and named it Mecklenburg. The town, now called Shepherdstown, is the oldest in the state.

When West Virginia's statehood bill was being written, it was decided that after July 4, 1863, all slaves in West Virginia over 21 years of age would be freed.

Industrialization in the late 1800s and early 1900s encouraged many African Americans to move to West Virginia for work.

West Virginia has a population density of about 28 people per square mile.

POPULATION

West Virginia is the thirty-fourth most populated state in the country. There are more than 1.8 million people living in the state. Most people in West Virginia are between 18 and 44 years old.

More than 96 percent of West Virginians are of European heritage, while slightly more than 3 percent are African American. The remaining 1 percent of the population is made up of Native Americans, Asians, and Hispanic Americans. The state has recently experienced a slight drop in population. The drop is a combination of a low **birthrate** and the migration of people out of the state. West Virginia's average birthrate of 11.4 births per 1,000 people is far below the national average of 14.6 births per 1,000 people.

West Virginia's Eastern Panhandle offers residents a combination of modern living and beautiful scenery.

At 293 feet, the Capitol dome in Charleston is the largest in the nation.

QUICK FACTS

African Americans won the right to vote in West Virginia in 1869. They also won the right to hold public office.

Democrats have dominated West Virginian politics since the Great Depression of the 1930s.

In 1885, it was decided that Charleston would be the state capital. Until then, the capital had been shuttled back and forth between Wheeling and Charleston.

Wheeling's Oglebay Park

West Virginia is divided into fifty-five counties, and each county has an elected board of citizens who represent the interests of that county.

POLITICS AND GOVERNMENT

West Virginia's government is divided into three branches—the executive, the legislative, and the judicial. The executive branch administers the laws, the legislative branch makes the laws, and the judicial branch enforces and interprets the laws. All of the branches are elected by the people of West Virginia.

The executive branch is headed by a governor elected for a four-year term. The governor is responsible for proposing the state budget, for appointing state department directors, and for signing bills into laws. The state's legislature has a Senate with thirty-four members and a House of Delegates with one hundred members.

The Kanawha County Courthouse was built in 1892.

CULTURAL GROUPS

West Virginia's distinct mountain culture is celebrated throughout the state. Musical ballads, gospel songs, and clog dancing are all part of this mountain heritage. Many of the mountain folk songs are of British or German origin. Mountain culture is also featured in outdoor dramas like *Honey in the Rock* and *The Hatfields and McCoys*.

The Augusta Heritage Center in the Potomac Highlands keeps the spirit of West Virginia's mountain Appalachian culture alive by offering classes in log-house building, fiddle and banjo playing, Celtic stone carving, and local Native-American, Irish, and Cajun storytelling. The center is called "Augusta" because most of the area that is now West Virginia was known as Augusta County, Virginia, before West Virginia became a separate state.

Students at the Augusta Heritage Center can practice the art of blacksmithing by learning how to make and use metal tools.

The Augusta Heritage Center teaches old-time banjo playing. The banjo is a popular traditional folk instrument in West Virginia.

QUICK FACTS

The legend of John Henry, "the steel drivin' man," comes from the small town of Talcott in southern West Virginia. Storytellers say that John could hammer like no one else and that he was even faster than a hammer drill machine.

West Virginia's first church was built near Bunker Hill in 1740.

Charles Town, in the Shenandoah Valley, was named in honor of George Washington's youngest brother, Charles. He gave many acres of land to the growing village and named many of the streets in the town.

The town of Helvetia was modeled after the architecture of Switzerland.

Deep in the heart of the Potomac Valley's Randolph County is a small community established by Swiss immigrants. They named their town Helvetia in honor of their homeland. *Helvetia* means "Switzerland" in Latin. The town still has an Alpine community and the Swiss-German **dialect** can often be heard in the streets. The community celebrates its heritage with such events as Swiss Independence Day and the Helvetia Fair.

West Virginia recognizes and celebrates the cultural heritage of the state's coal-mining industry. Since coal was discovered in southern West Virginia in 1742 along the Coal River, more than 4 billion tons have been mined from these historic coal fields. Visitors to the Beckley Exhibition Coal Mines can explore some of the 1,500 feet of underground passages, ride in an underground coal car, and experience what the lives of West Virginia's rugged miners might have been like.

Since 1962, retired miners serving as tour guides have taken visitors into the caves of the Beckley coal mines. A miniature electric locomotive pulls tourists into the mines to teach them about mining history.

Jamboree USA broadcasts live from the Capitol Music Hall in Wheeling.

ARTS AND ENTERTAINMENT

There has always been a love of bluegrass, old-time, and country music in West Virginia. The music capital of the state is Wheeling, where the live-radio country music show, *Jamboree USA*, is broadcast to devoted listeners. It is the second-oldest live-radio show in the United States.

West Virginia's strong country music roots have produced many singing stars. Kathy Mattea is a West Virginian who won the Female Vocalist of the Year award twice at the Country Music Association Awards. She has recorded more than ten studio albums and has enjoyed enormous fan support, along with many number-one hits.

Born in South Charleston, Kathy Mattea grew up with the influences of folk and bluegrass music. Her style of music reflects her West Virginian upbringing. She even wrote a song called "Leavin' West Virginia."

Billie Holiday was nicknamed the Lady, or Lady Day, for her majestic charm. She sang in clubs in Parkersburg and Charleston.

One of West Virginia's most well-known writers is Pearl S. Buck, who won the Pulitzer Prize in 1932 for her book *The Good Earth*. Buck also won the Nobel Prize for Literature and is the only woman from the United States to win both awards. She was born and raised in Hillsboro, which is part of West Virginia's Pocahontas County.

There have been some talented actors and comedians to come out of West Virginia. One of the most notable West Virginian comedians is Don Knotts. Knotts went to school at West Virginia University as a speech major. Originally, he intended to pursue a career in teaching. This Morgantown native found great success on television, as well as in films. He became well known for his Emmy Award-winning role as Barney Fife on *The Andy Griffith Show*. He made audiences laugh as the crazy landlord on the television show *Three's Company*. Knotts also starred in numerous movies, including *The Incredible Mr. Limpet*, *Shakiest Gun in the West*, *Gus*, *Cannonball Run II*, and *Pleasantville*.

QUICK FACTS

Billie Holiday is considered one of the best female jazz singers of all time. She spent some time in West Virginia in the late 1940s. Billie sang with the Artie Shaw Orchestra in both Parkersburg and Charleston in June of 1938. Billie Holiday was the first African-American singer to lead a non-African-American band.

Many of the most important playwrights from the United States are showcased at the month-long Contemporary American Theater Festival at Shepherd College in Shepherdstown.

In June, the Greenbrier Valley Festival of the Arts is held in Lewisburg. Local artists and musicians gather to present a weekend of world-class entertainment.

During World War II, Don Knotts toured the Pacific Islands as a comedian in a show called "Stars and Gripes."

SPORTS

Race-car driving in the Shenandoah Valley is very popular, even with movie stars. Both Paul Newman and Tom Cruise are regular visitors to West Virginia's Summit Point Raceway. It is a 2-mile course that covers more than 375 acres. It is considered one of the most challenging racetracks in the nation. The raceway hosts Sports Car Club of America events for professional and amateur auto racing, as well as motorcycle and go-cart races.

West Virginia has also had success in gymnastics. Olympic gymnast Mary Lou Retton was born in Fairmont in 1968. She won five medals at the 1984 Summer Olympics in Los Angeles. She was the first person from the United States to ever win a gold medal in Olympic gymnastics.

Summit Point Raceway's ten-turn road challenge offers more than just race-car driving. It also offers lessons in accident avoidance, police driving, and security driving.

QUICK FACTS

Canaan Valley is considered to have some of the best skiing in the mid-Atlantic states. The valley has six resorts to accommodate skiers. Snow in the valley often lasts well into the spring.

Charleston has a dog track where enthusiasts can watch some of the best greyhound racing in the country.

On October 14, 1947, Charles "Chuck" Elwood Yeager became the first person to fly faster than the speed of sound. He broke the sound barrier while flying the experimental Bell X-1. He also became the first person to fly more than twice the speed of sound. Yeager was born at Myra in Lincoln County.

Mary Lou Retton was just 7 years old when she started taking gymnastics classes at West Virginia University.

QUICK FACTS

Charles Town is a popular spot for thoroughbred horse racing. The Charles Town Races have been running since 1786.

The first bareknuckle world heavyweight boxing championship was held on June 1, 1880, near Colliers. Paddy Ryan of Ireland won the title by knocking out Joe Goss of England in the eighty-fifth round.

West Virginian baseball player George Brett was one of the Kansas City Royals' biggest stars. He was a thirteen-time All-Star and was named the League's Player of the Week a record twelve times. Brett was inducted into the Baseball Hall of Fame in 1999.

West Virginia is home to a number of popular yet unusual sports. Rock climbers from around the nation come to the Potomac Highlands to climb the incredible sandstone formations known as the Seneca Rocks.

Woodchopping is another unusual sport that is practiced in West Virginia. A back-breaking competition is held yearly at the Webster County Woodchopping Festival. The rugged and difficult life of the lumberjack is celebrated by competitors from around the world.

West Virginia has excellent white-water rafting along some of its wilder rivers. In the Gauley River National Recreational Area there are some difficult rapids, whose names include "Heaven Help You" and "Lost Paddle."

The Woodchopping Festival attracts international athletes for a two-day competition in May. It is one of the most renowned chopping competitions in the world.

The fact that West Virginia has the highest average elevation of any state east of the Mississippi River makes it a rock climber's paradise.

Brain Teasers

1 Shenandoah is a Native-American word which means:

a. "Daughter of the Mountains"

b. "Daughter of the Valley"

c. "Daughter of the Skies"

d. "Daughter of Denver"

Answer: c. "Daughter of the Skies"

2 In what county did the Golden Delicious apple originate?

Answer: The Golden Delicious apple originated in Clay County. The original Golden apple tree was discovered in 1775 near Wellsburg.

3 Which city in West Virginia is known as the "Nail City"?

Answer: The city of Wheeling became known as the Nail City because of its iron production.

4 Harpers Ferry National Historical Park is located in which area of West Virginia?

a. Ohio River Valley

b. Potomac Highlands

c. Eastern Panhandle

d. Shenandoah Valley

Answer: c. Eastern Panhandle

5 What is the town of Grafton known for?

Answer: Andrews Church in Grafton was the first place in the world to celebrate Mother's Day on May 10, 1908.

6 Who launched the first steamboat?

Answer: On December 3, 1787, James Rumsey launched the first steamboat on the Potomac River. A large crowd gathered on the banks to watch.

7 Which family feud started over a pig?

Answer: The Hatfield-McCoy feud between West Virginia and Kentucky began in 1882 over the theft of a pig. The feud lasted for nearly thirty years and resulted in the death of twelve people.

8 Who was Punch Jones?

Answer: Punch Jones was the name given to the diamond found in Peterstown. The diamond was named after Grover and Punch Jones, who discovered it. It was valued at more than $100,000.

FOR MORE INFORMATION

Books

Rice, Otis K. *The Mountain State: An Introduction to West Virginia*. Charleston: West Virginia Historical Education Foundation, 1997.

Williams, John Alexander. *West Virginia: A History for Beginners*. Charleston: Appalachian Editions, 1993.

The World Almanac and Book of Facts 2001. Cleveland: World Almanac, 2000.

Web sites

You can also go online and have a look at the following Web sites:

State of West Virginia
http://www.state.wv.us/

West Virginia Web
http://wvweb.com

West Virginia State Parks and Forests
http://www.wvparks.com

Some Web sites stay current longer than others. To find other West Virginia Web sites, enter search terms such as "West Virginia," "Charleston," "Harpers Ferry," or any other topic you want to research.

GLOSSARY

abolitionist: someone who wants to put an end to slavery

alliance: a union

archeologists: scientists who study early peoples through artifacts and remains

artisans: highly skilled crafts people

birthrate: the number of births compared to the total population

bituminous coal: a type of soft coal that burns with a smoky flame

broiler chickens: chickens raised for their meat rather than their eggs

chestnut blight: a disease that attacks chestnut trees

dialect: a particular variety of a language, usually specific to a geographic area

fabricated metals: metals that are manufactured, such as steel

hybrids: combinations of two different plants

mean altitude: the average height above sea level

median age: where exactly half of the population is older than a given age, and the other half is younger

migratory: moving from one place to another

quarried: stone removed from an excavation pit

rural: relating to the country; farming based

sediment: minerals and organic matter that are deposited by water or ice

treaties: formal agreements between two parties

tributaries: small streams or rivers that feed into larger bodies of water